THE FOREST IN THE SEA

Seaweed Solutions to Planetary Problems

Anita Sanchez

books for a better earth™

holiday house • new york

This is for you, Laine

The publisher wishes to thank Dr. Abigail Tyrell
for her expert review of the text.

A **Books for a Better Earth**™ Title

The Books for a Better Earth™ collection is designed to inspire young people to become active, knowledgeable participants in caring for the planet they live on. Focusing on solutions to climate change challenges, the collection looks at how scientists, activists, and young leaders are working to safeguard Earth's future.

Library of Congress Cataloging-in-Publication Data
Names: Sanchez, Anita, 1956- author.
Title: The forest in the sea : seaweed solutions to planetary problems /
Anita Sanchez.
Description: First edition. | New York : Holiday House, [2023] | Series:
Books for a better earth | Includes bibliographical references.
Audience: Ages 8–12 | Audience: Grades 4–6 | Summary: "An exploration of
seaweed's role in marine ecosystems and climate change solutions" –
Provided by publisher.
Identifiers: LCCN 2022001752 | ISBN: 9780823450138 (hardcover)
Subjects: LCSH: Marine algae–Ecophysiology–Juvenile literature. | Marine
algae–Climatic factors–Juvenile literature. | Climate change mitigation–Juvenile literature.
Classification: LCC QK570.2 .S26 2023 | DDC 579.8/177–dc23/eng/20220126
LC record available at https://lccn.loc.gov/2022001752

ISBN: 978-0-8234-5013-8 (hardcover)
ISBN: 978-0-8234-5876-9 (paperback)

TABLE OF CONTENTS

INTRODUCTION:
WELCOME TO THE FOREST

You're walking along a beach in the warm sun. Blue sky, blue waves, bathing suit, flip-flops . . . sounds great, doesn't it? You look out to sea, admiring the sunset, hoping to see a whale. You don't look down at what's underfoot: just a lot of sand and some dried-up seaweed.

But those weeds you're walking over are worth a second glance. They're among the oldest forms of life on Earth, filled with mysterious secrets that scientists have yet to unlock. And they just might hold the key to our planet's future.

Meet an unlikely hero: the wet, slimy stuff known as seaweed.

A WORLD OF WATER

Beneath the sunlit surface of the waves lie some of the most amazing forests in the world. Forests where you can float weightlessly among schools of fish. Huge green pastures where sea turtles graze. Forests that capture carbon and breathe out oxygen. The

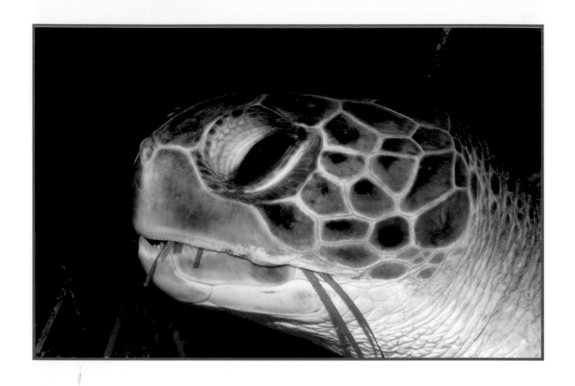

answers to many of our planet's problems may lie underwater, too, hidden in these forests of seaweed.

Our planet is undergoing a frightening change. Human-caused pollution is altering Earth's atmosphere and causing the planet to heat up. This global change affects the oceans as much as it affects the land. As ocean temperatures rise, ice caps melt, currents veer off course, and weather patterns change. We're feeling this already in rising sea levels, more powerful hurricanes that batter coasts, and droughts that cause deadly wildfires. Wildlife habitats are threatened, food shortages loom. There's a lot of environmental bad news these days, and dire problems lie ahead.

But there are solutions to be found under the waves.

No matter where you live—right by the ocean or far inland—

seaweed affects you, and every human on this planet. We all need food to eat, water to drink, and air to breathe. Seaweed gives us all those things—and more.

ONE
COWS IN THE FOREST

As you walk along the edge of the waves, you might expect to see some other creatures hanging out (besides humans). Some animals seem to belong on a beach: a gull, a seal, or a crab skittering for shelter beneath a pile of seaweed. You probably wouldn't expect to bump into a cow.

Joe Dorgan's dairy farm is located on remote Prince Edward Island, off the coast of Canada. The island is green and beautiful, edged with red-sand beaches and rocky cliffs. It's a great place for a summer swim—but the summers are short. In early fall, cold winds howl from the Arctic, and dark ocean waters pound the beach. It's a hard place to scratch out a living as a farmer.

Joe Dorgan's family farm is in a little town known as Seacow Pond. On a tight budget, Joe was looking for a way to keep his herd of dairy cows healthy. Most farmers buy feed additives filled with artificial chemicals to pump up their cows' nutrition so that they'll give more milk. But Joe had a frustratingly hard time finding any

inexpensive, natural feeds with the high level of nutrition dairy cows need.

And then he remembered, long ago when he was a boy, walking with his father on the beach and helping him gather the red, ruffled **fronds** of a seaweed called Irish moss.

Joe's grandfather came from Ireland, and the family had always used seaweed to fertilize gardens. They would lug heavy buckets of damp seaweed up to the garden plots, and shovel it

into the soil of the potato patch. "All my life I've been at the Irish moss," Joe remembers. "Our dad had us hauling [seaweed] off of the beach to grow his potatoes. It's good fertilizer, it's good animal feed, it's good for people, it's good for everything."

Hidden beneath the roiling gray surface of the ocean are forests of Irish moss growing in the cold water. Thick bunches of it,

mixed with other species of seaweed, cling tightly to rocks, but winter storms can rip seaweed loose. Crashing waves hurl it onto the beach, where it lies on the sand in heaps. "There's a mixture of Irish moss, rockweed, and kelp, and just going to waste," Joe says. "And I knew it was good because years ago our ancestors, that's what they done their business with." Joe Dorgan began collecting

Seaweed Close-Up: Irish Moss (Chondrus crispus)

Ruffles of lacy Irish moss are found on cold, rocky coasts around the North Atlantic from Europe to Iceland to Maine. It's not only food for cows—people have been eating it for centuries. When simmered with milk, it thickens into a Jell-O-like pudding that's bland-tasting but very nutritious.

Irish moss is used today to make a substance called carrageenan, which is used by the commercial food industry as a cheap and easy way to thicken watery foods. It's commonly found in soups, pudding, and many other things, including toothpaste.

If putting seaweed in food sounds surprising to you, check the label on the next carton of ice cream you buy—chances are you've been eating seaweed for years.

more of this bounty, delivered for free by the waves.

After the seaweed was dried and brittle, he ground it up into powder and sprinkled it on his cows' food. And just as his grandfather's lore had promised, his cows became healthier. The seaweed-eating cows were more energetic. Their fur was smooth and glossy, and they put on weight. They produced more creamy, delicious milk (which did *not* taste like seaweed). The cows also gave birth to more calves, and the calves were healthier, too.

Joe Dorgan was curious. Why did a sprinkling of seaweed have such a powerful effect on his cows? He wanted to explore the mystery further.

So he took some samples of his seaweed feed to a chemist on the faculty of nearby Dalhousie University. Dr. Robert Kinley analyzed the seaweed, but he was baffled, too. He couldn't put his finger on why it had such a strong effect on the animals. True, it contained surprisingly high amounts of vitamins and minerals, but so did the store-bought artificial supplements. What

was the special magic of seaweed?

Joe Dorgan and Robert Kinley are just two of the people who are trying to find out the secrets of seaweed—and realizing that there's more to this stuff than meets the eye. What other surprises does seaweed have in store?

Before we dive deeper into their research, let's explore seaweed forests around the world, to understand some of the amazing roles that seaweed plays on our planet. To begin with, we'll try to figure out a very important and complicated mystery, one that baffled the earliest scientists and is still perplexing the experts today: What *is* seaweed, anyway?

Seaweed Science: Seaweed-Eating Sheep

On North Ronaldsay, an island off the coast of Scotland, lives a flock of sheep that eat seaweed—and only seaweed. The remote, rocky island has almost no grass growing on it, and the sheep that have grazed there for centuries have adapted to eating seaweed—and now they can't easily digest grass, hay, or other normal sheep foods.

The seaweed-loving sheep clamber over the slippery, wet rocks, grazing on rockweed and sea lettuce. They'll even swim to areas of tastier seaweed. When the seaweed is covered at high tide, the sheep wait, chewing their seaweed cuds, and at low tide they return to the beaches to feed.

Sadly, their seaweed-rimmed island is at risk. As climate change warms our planet, glaciers and ice caps melt, raising the level of water in the oceans. Climate change also brings more powerful storms and increasingly heavy rainfall to grind away sand and soil, eroding the island's coastline at an ever-increasing rate. North Ronaldsay is only a few feet above sea level.

TWO
THE DANCING FOREST

Long streamers of the seaweed called dulse float in the waves like red ribbons. Emerald-green sea lettuce sprouts in short, fat bunches like cabbage. Golden crayweed forms dense forests on shallow rocks, constantly shoved back and forth by waves.

There are thousands of species of seaweed, in a bewildering variety of colors, shapes, and sizes. The massive seaweed called bull kelp can grow as tall as land trees, a hundred feet or more, stretching toward the sun from beneath the waves. Other species are made up of single floating cells. Some look like plants, some look like rocks, and some look like piles of tangled string. Scientists have been arguing for centuries over exactly what these wet, weedy life forms are.

Seaweed looks like a plant, but it's neither plant nor animal nor fungus. It's a whole separate form of life: **algae**. There are three main types of algae, named for their colors: red, green, and brown. Most biologists use the general term "seaweed" for the plantlike forms of algae that live in salt water.

LONG BEFORE THE DINOSAURS

Algae were one of the first forms of life to appear in the shallow, mineral-rich seas that covered the earth billions of years ago. First came one-celled organisms floating in the water, then over the long, slow passage of time those first specks of algae evolved into more complex, multi-celled life forms.

Scientists have discovered tiny fossils of a green alga called *Proterocladus antiquus*, only two millimeters long (about half the size of a popcorn kernel). The fossils were embedded in rock layers that had once been an ancient sea, a billion years ago. So seaweed was already an ancient life form millions of years before dinosaurs appeared. Sharks were swimming through seaweed eons before birds were singing in trees.

Many biologists agree that all the plants we know on land—grass, trees, moss, ferns, lettuce, petunias—evolved from green algae. And

Seaweed Science: Classification

Take a deep breath before plunging into the complicated subject of seaweed classification! In the 1700s, a scientist named Carolus Linnaeus divided all living things into two categories that he called kingdoms: *Plantae* and *Animalia*. Seaweed plainly wasn't an animal, he reasoned, so it must be a plant. In the centuries since Linnaeus, scientists have discovered that seaweed is a bit more complicated than that.

Over the years, the development of better microscopes showed that algae have cells that are very different from the cells of plants. In the twentieth century, scientists learned about DNA and how to use it to figure out which organisms are related to each other.

So seaweeds have mostly been ousted from the plant kingdom—but where to put them? Scientists have had to create whole new kingdoms to sort out the bewildering variety of life that's being discovered. Biologists still debate exactly how to classify seaweed, and it's an ongoing process. In the twenty-first century, many marine algae are considered to be in the kingdom Protista, based on the inner structure of their cells.

seaweed was lying on the beach long, long before the earliest ancestors of modern humans evolved, about five million years ago. Seaweed was here first, and it's still around.

Seaweed Science: How Low Can You Go?

Since all seaweeds need sunlight to grow, they can only survive where the sun can reach. The top layer of ocean water, where sunlight can easily penetrate, is called the **photic zone.** How deep that is can vary, since it depends on how clear the water is. In water that's cloudy, little light can get through. In crystal-clear water, sunlight can penetrate five hundred feet or more.

Green algae tend to grow in the uppermost layers of the water, but brown algae can grow farther down. Red algae can survive even in very low light levels, down in the dark water where only a few gleams of sunlight can penetrate. A few types of red algae can exist at more than five hundred feet deep.

PLANTS VERSUS ALGAE

Seaweeds manufacture their own food through the chemical process known as **photosynthesis,** using sunlight and carbon dioxide to make sugars that nourish them. Green plants do that, too. Many seaweeds look like plants, with parts that seem to be leaves, branches, or roots. But seaweed is as different from land plants as a bird is from a fish.

To begin with, seaweed doesn't have roots. Most plants use a huge amount of energy to grow a network of roots, thrusting their way through soil in the endless quest for water. But there's no need for roots to suck up water if you're floating in it! Seaweed just absorbs all the moisture it needs from the sea that surrounds it. Some seaweeds float free in the water, but species of seaweed that attach to rocks or the ocean floor have parts called **holdfasts.** These might look like roots, or little claws, or suction cups, but they're just holding on to the surface, not absorbing anything.

Land plants tend to grow a stiff spine to hold them up tall and straight. Since they need sunlight to make food, they need strong stems to support their weight as they reach toward the sky. A tree

uses most of its energy building a massive trunk to hold up all those food-making leaves. But most seaweed just drifts lazily, using the buoyancy of water. Some seaweeds, like rockweed, get an extra lift from air-filled bubbles called bladders, and a few do have stiff skeletons.

Many types of plants also grow a vascular system: a network of tubes to carry water and food from the roots to the leaves and back again (like human veins carrying blood all over our bodies). But seawater is a rich soup of **nutrients**, the chemicals that living things need to survive: iron, calcium, potassium, and many more. Only the hugest seaweeds, like the kelp that grows off the California coast, bother with growing a tube system. Most seaweeds just suck up whatever they need straight from seawater.

So seaweed is a very efficient form of life. No need to waste energy on roots and stems and leaves. Some kinds, like giant

kelp, can grow eighteen inches in a single day! Seaweed is really good at growing—growing big, growing more, growing fast.

THE FOREST ECOSYSTEM

A food chain is simple: little fish are eaten by big fish, which are eaten by bigger fish, and so forth. An ecosystem is far more complex. It includes all the living things in an area, from the hugest whales to the tiniest speck of algae. It also includes the nonliving parts of the environment: water, sunlight, rocks, and climate.

Seaweed is the basis of all marine ecosystems, the start of all the food chains in the ocean. It's essential to countless species of wildlife. Some creatures spend their entire lives in seaweed—eating it, hiding in it, clinging to it, laying eggs in it. Other creatures use seaweed as nurseries: safe places where the young ones can grow, hidden among the sheltering fronds.

A seaweed forest is a very strange place, if you're used to life on land. Have you ever been in a forest where the trees lay themselves flat on the ground every few hours, and then rise again? Seems too bizarre to be real—but that's exactly what the rockweed forest does.

A COLLAPSING FOREST

Usually, we see seaweed after it's dead—just a tangle of dried-out weeds scattered across the beach where the waves have tossed

it. But once we leave the beach and peer beneath the waves, it's a different story. Living seaweed dances with the motion of the sea, bending gracefully in the water. It's alive and active—making food, growing, breathing.

Imagine putting on a mask and snorkel to enter one of these underwater forests, in the cold, clear waters of the North Atlantic. It's high tide, and waves are lapping on the granite rocks of the Massachusetts coast. Even with a wet suit, you can't stay too long in this icy water—already the chill is seeping into your skin. But linger for a minute and watch: this cold underwater forest is filled with life.

The seaweed below you is massed in huge clumps, mostly made up of long strands of a species called brown rockweed. You're like a bird flying over treetops, gazing down on seaweed fronds moving to the rhythm of the ocean waves.

The rockweed is home to a whole world of wildlife: fish, lobsters, snails, tiny shrimp, spiny sea urchins like purple pincushions. Constellations of pink starfish are scattered across the rocks, and a green crab scutters along the sandy bottom. Dark blue shellfish called mussels cling to the rocks, their shells open as they suck in seawater and small bits of food. There's so much to see, you could stay in this forest for hours, but your teeth are starting to chatter. Time to warm up in the sun.

Now watch closely as the seaweed forest folds itself up.

Rockweed is a kind of seaweed that grows only in the intertidal zone, the area between the levels of high and low tides. Every six hours, the tide changes. During the ebb tide, when the sea level drops, the seaweed sinks lower and lower, too. Finally the tide is at its lowest, and the rockweed is laid out flat on the sand or draped over the rocks. Now you can walk where just a few short hours ago fish were swimming.

The shore at low tide has a weedy, fishy smell. It seems lifeless, nothing but sand and rocks covered with limp, brown weeds. But the rockweed forest is still filled with life. Lift up a wet handful of rockweed, and there they are: barnacles, starfish, urchins, crabs, all protected against the hot, drying sun by their thick wet blanket. And there are smaller organisms, too, ones you can hardly see:

thousands of insects, shrimp, and tiny buglike creatures called amphipods, hiding in the tangle.

Now come the seabirds: gulls, terns, ducks, and many more. They hunt through the wet weed for a bounty of food. Sometimes mammals like foxes or raccoons paw through the seaweed for tasty crabs and shrimp. People might come, too, to search for delicious mussels hidden under the wet blanket.

But soon the sea comes trickling back. The land creatures retreat, as it's time for the rockweed forest to rise again.

Seaweed gives life by providing food and shelter. But it also nurtures life in a way we can't see. Seaweed is not only good at growing—it's incredibly good at producing oxygen.

One of the most amazing forests on Earth is the one we'll visit next. Unlike the rockweed clinging to the rocky shore, this forest floats free, in the remotest parts of the deep ocean. It's an odd

Seaweed Close-Up: Rockweed (*Ascophyllum nodosum*)

Rockweed, sea lettuce, wrack, and many other types of seaweed live in the intertidal zone. For hours, they're totally submerged in salt water, and then for hours they're baking on a rock in the hot sun. A fish or a dandelion or a person couldn't survive that!

Rockweed manages this crazy lifestyle because its fronds contain algin, a jellylike substance. While the rockweed is submerged, the algin absorbs water like a sponge, holding the wetness as the tide slips away. Although the outer skin of the seaweed may be dry and crusty, inside it's moist enough to last until the tide turns.

forest—no roots, no branches, just trillions of tiny bits of green bobbing in the blue waves.

You could say that this is the mightiest forest in the world, because it creates an incredible amount of the air we need to breathe—more oxygen than all the planet's land forests put together.

THREE
THE WANDERING FOREST

A giant whale dives into the blackness of the deep ocean. Powerful fins and a massive tail power the whale's body down through the midnight-dark water. The whale is hunting.

After eating huge mouthfuls, the whale slowly rises. There's a *whoosh!* as the long-held breath lets go. The whale drifts on the surface of the water, digesting its meal. And not long afterward, the whale does what every living thing does after eating—it poops. Let's be scientific and say it excretes. A jet of brownish gunk squirts out of the whale's anus. Whale poop doesn't sink, it floats on the water. The whole thing is pretty smelly, as you can imagine: fishy, gross, and disgusting. You certainly wouldn't want to take a swim anywhere near where a whale has done its business.

But whale poop isn't pollution—it's fertilizer.

OCEAN FERTILIZER

Imagine a farmer growing corn. The farmer plows the field, and plants the seeds—simple, right? But it's more complex than that.

To ensure a good crop, the farmer has to put some fertilizer on the corn. Fertilizer is anything that's added to plants to give them essential nutrients they need to build their cells, like iron, nitrogen, and potassium. Nitrogen is one of the most important, since most soil doesn't have much of it.

In the ocean, it works the same way. But there's no corn growing in the ocean waves. Instead, there are microscopic bits of seaweed called **phytoplankton**.

Each tiny speck of phytoplankton has no roots, no stems, no leaves—it's just a little green floating dot. It's hard to wrap your mind around how small one single organism of phytoplankton is. A million of them could fit in a teaspoon, with room left over. It's almost impossible to glimpse one all by itself, and you need a

microscope attached to your camera to take a picture of one. But when billions of them float together, they turn the sea green. Phytoplankton forests wander over the surface of the ocean, bobbing in the waves, pushed by currents and winds.

A WATERY DESERT

On a map or a globe, the ocean is shown as all solid blue. But just as land ecosystems aren't the same—a rain forest is different from a desert—the sea isn't the same all the world over. Some areas of the sea are ten times as salty as other parts. Some waters are bathwater warm, some are freezing cold with icebergs floating in them. Some sections of the ocean are rich with all the nutrients plants need—and some are not.

Just like the corn plants struggling to grow in the farmer's field, phytoplankton need fertilizer: iron, potassium, and especially nitrogen. But there's no farmer with a tractor spreading manure out on the briny deep. Fortunately, there are whales. A big blast of whale poop is packed with exactly the stuff that phytoplankton need to grow.

Wait a minute—why has it got to be whales? There are surely other creatures pooping in the ocean—why can't they fertilize the phytoplankton?

The reason is that whales tend to feed deep in the ocean, but must return to the surface to breathe. Sperm whales dive a mile or more down, hunting squid and other creatures that live only in the dark depths. Humpbacks swim deep to feed on sand eels. Giant blue whales dive five hundred feet down to slurp up tiny shrimp-like crustaceans called **krill**.

Then the whales rise, carrying a huge load of nutrients in their massive stomachs. They excrete their waste on the surface. Then

Seaweed Close-Up: Phytoplankton

Scientists are still figuring out exactly what those green specks are, but they know that they're not all the same species. The most common type of phytoplankton is photosynthetic bacteria. Some are single-celled specks of algae in the kingdom *Protista*. Whatever they're called, phytoplankton are on the menu for all sorts of creatures, from whales to tiny floating shrimplike creatures called zooplankton.

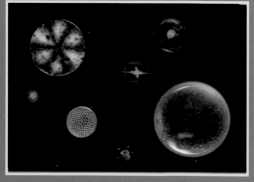

Far out in the open ocean, where the phytoplankton roam, there are few nutrients in the water. That's not the case near the coast. The shallow water near the shore is nature's seaweed farm. Along the coasts of continents, winds and currents bump into the land and push surface water aside. Deeper water then flows upward to replace the water that's been displaced, in a process called upwelling. Deep water is rich in nutrients, so the surge of rising water carries a big blast of fertilizer.

Also near the coast, rivers and streams bring runoff from chemical fertilizers used on land. This makes the water really fertile—a good thing, you'd think. But too much seaweed is as bad as too little. Beware of harmful algal blooms, aka HABs!

HABs happen when there are *too many* nutrients in the water and too much algae grows too fast. Bacteria start to consume the algae, which eventually lowers the oxygen in the water. HABs can suffocate massive numbers of fish and shellfish. Some HABs even create toxins in the water that can harm people as well as wildlife. Massive growths of red-colored algae can make water turn red, called a "red tide."

it's back down to the depths to feed again. Up and down, again and again. Marine biologists call this pattern the "whale pump."

It's a complete circle, a cycle— nature's way of moving things from one place to another, from the ocean depths to the surface. Without the whales, huge amounts of nitrogen and other key nutrients would just settle to the ocean floor and stay there. These giant marine mammals are a crucial part of the deep ocean ecosystem—the very heart of it, in fact, endlessly pumping the ingredients for life through the water.

GREEN WATER, CLEAN AIR

All phytoplankton are **autotrophs**, which means they create their own food. Just like a corn plant on land, each speck of phytoplankton is making food. The process of photosynthesis creates oxygen, which is released into our atmosphere—and trillions of phytoplankton crank out an unbelievable amount of oxygen. Almost half of the oxygen in Earth's atmosphere comes from oceanic phytoplankton.

Think about it. Every other breath you take comes from seaweed.

The second good thing that happens during all this plankton food-making is that carbon dioxide is removed from the atmosphere. CO_2 is one of the main pollutants that cause the worst effects of climate change. Human activities, like driving cars and burning oil and coal in power plants, pump billions of tons of CO_2 into the air.

Lucky for us humans that phytoplankton grow so abundantly and reproduce so fast. They can double their numbers in a few days—but only if they get the nutrients they need. Whales probably don't realize it, but with every poop they're not only fertilizing phytoplankton, they're fighting climate change.

More and more, we're realizing how much every living thing

Seaweed Science: Photosynthesis

Let's take a deep dive into a single cell of phytoplankton. It's as green as a blade of grass because both contain chlorophyll, a green-colored chemical that absorbs the sun's energy to power photosynthesis.

Here's how it works. The phytoplankton cell, bobbing in a sunlit wave, absorbs water (H_2O) from the sea it's floating in, and sucks carbon dioxide (CO_2) from the air or water. Then it breaks these molecules apart, turning them into a type of carbon-based sugar that it can use for food. But the phytoplankton doesn't need all of the oxygen (O_2), so the extra O_2 is released from the cell—giving the air more oxygen for us all to breathe!

on our planet depends on seaweed. The next forest we'll explore is filled with a huge variety of creatures whose lives are totally intertwined with the weedy forest they live in. The seaweed forms a giant cradle for some of the most incredible babies in the ocean, floating in a mysterious place of legends and sea monsters called the Sargasso Sea.

FOUR
THE UPSIDE-DOWN FOREST

The Sargasso Sea isn't a sea of water—it's a vast golden sea of seaweed. It's an area of the Atlantic Ocean of nearly two million square miles (about half the size of the United States) covered with dense mats of a floating seaweed called sargassum.

Sargassum has air-filled bladders, which act like water wings to keep the seaweed afloat for its entire life. Its fronds hang down into the water of the Sargasso, which is almost as calm as a lake, but very deep—the bottom in places lies nearly three miles below the quiet surface. Sargassum drifts endlessly, never needing to touch the land.

Why does all this seaweed hang out in the middle of the ocean? The Sargasso region is surrounded by powerful currents that swirl like water around the drain of a sink. The force of the currents pulls the seaweed masses into the center of the spiral, trapping them there.

Seaweed Close-Up: Sargassum
(Sargassum natans, Sargassum fluitans)

These two closely related seaweeds are the main species that float in the Sargasso Sea. Like trees, some individual sargassums can live for decades, and some keep growing for a century or more.

Each frond looks like the long thin branch of a tree, but it isn't stiff like wood—it's more like rubber, soft and flexible.

Occasional clumps of this drifting seaweed have always escaped the currents and drifted to beaches in Florida, the Caribbean, and as far away as North Africa. But since 2011, enormous mats of sargassum have invaded beaches in summer. The masses of seaweed are sometimes too thick for swimmers to get into the water. Sea turtles can't reach the sand to lay eggs. The seaweed isn't toxic, but mounds of it decompose into a smelly mess that sends tourists fleeing and can cause fish kills. Cleanup can cost millions of dollars.

Why this sudden, enormous invasion of sargassum? Seawater is warmed by climate change, and also polluted with fertilizers from huge, industrial-size farms and ranches. Droughts in places as far away as the Sahara Desert are causing erosion, and the wind-blown soil ends up in the ocean, adding to the nutrient load. And once again: *too many nutrients equals too much seaweed.*

Europeans who sailed through the Sargasso Sea in the fifteenth century were astounded to see seaweed floating so far from land. They feared their wooden sailing ships would be stuck in the tangled weeds, stranding them in the middle of the ocean. Those sailors' tales of swirling tentacles of seaweed spawned centuries of legends about sea monsters. The western region of the Sargasso, the infamous Bermuda Triangle, is a place of mystery to this day. It's rumored to be a place where ships and planes and even people mysteriously disappear—perhaps eaten by sea monsters that lurk in the deep, weedy water.

And it's true that there are bizarre creatures, millions of them, lurking in the sargassum—but most of them are very, very small.

A GOLDEN FLOATING RAIN FOREST

When you look down toward the water from the deck of a ship, sargassum looks like flat, floating mats of weed. But below the surface is a whole forest—upside down.

Seaweed Science: Plastic Pollution

When those long-ago sailors peered nervously down from their ships, they were fearful of seeing terrible things. All they saw was seaweed. But if you looked at the Sargasso Sea today, you would see something terrible indeed: plastic.

The same currents that sweep tons of seaweed into the Sargasso also carry tons of floating plastic litter. Plastic takes a long time to break down and decompose—perhaps centuries. Billions of pieces of plastic trash bob among the sargassum, creating a monster indeed: a dreadful floating island called the "Great Atlantic Garbage Patch."

Animals get tangled in the plastic, or eat colorful bits of litter, which can injure or even kill them. Sea turtles swallow plastic bags, mistaking them for jellyfish. Seabirds eat brightly colored bottle caps and fishing lures. Whales die with their stomachs clogged with plastic.

How can we keep plastic out of the ocean? Picking up litter and recycling are important, of course. But we also need to find ways to eliminate plastics made from oil, which can take centuries to decompose.

Chemists are finding ways to create biodegradable plastics, which break down harmlessly when exposed to air and sun. Bioplastics are made out of organic materials (things that were once alive), including all sorts of unlikely ingredients: orange peels, potatoes, sawdust, corn. And it turns out one of the best materials for making bioplastics is . . . seaweed! Many companies all over the world are producing plastic bags, cups, straws, spoons, and bottles made from seaweed.

Think of a forest, with trees reaching up from the ground, spreading branches high into the air. Now flip that picture, and imagine trees hanging down from the sky. That's what it's like in the sargassum forest. Sheltered in the downward-hanging fronds of seaweed is a complex, layered ecosystem as rich as the one found in a tropical rain forest.

In that deep ocean where there are no rocks to cling to, the seaweed becomes the land. Strands of golden weed are crusted with barnacles, sponges, and tube worms, the kinds of creatures that usually cling to rocks. Some small creatures, like crabs, stay on their seaweed patch, living their whole lives on a tiny floating island.

Living in the Sargasso are many species found nowhere else in the world. They match the seaweed precisely and are almost invisible in it. If you're a sea creature who is small, defenseless, and tasty, the best way to survive is to blend in with whatever is all around you. The sargasso fish, named for the seaweed it lives in, looks exactly like a floating bit of weed. Protected from predators, the sargasso fish uses fingerlike fins to wriggle through the seaweed, preying on even smaller fish.

UNDERWATER KINDERGARTEN

Many small creatures, especially young ones, use the upside-down forest as a nursery—a place to grow safely, protected from predators. Baby sea turtles, after hatching on land, travel hundreds of miles to reach the Sargasso and grow up in its protection. They'll hide in the shelter of the forest until they grow big enough to have a chance of survival in open water.

Eels are water creatures that look like snakes, but they're really just a skinny kind of fish. They live in freshwater ponds and streams, sometimes for years, but they always return to the Sargasso, where they were spawned. No one knows how eels find their way to their birthplace, hundreds of miles through the trackless sea.

Once sheltered by the thick seaweed, female eels lay millions of eggs. After hatching, baby eels hide in the sargassum for years before heading back to the land their parents came from.

The Sargasso Sea is also a giant playpen for baby fish. More than a hundred species of fish lay eggs there, and the babies hang out in the calm, warm water. Some fish live in the weed all their lives, like the pufferfish, which can inflate itself into a spiny porcupine when threatened. Others leave the forest once they have grown large enough to risk open water: tuna, swordfish, marlin. Many of these species are fish that the people of the world depend on for food.

Just as hawks hunt in the sky over a land forest, predators

hunt in the deep water beneath the seaweed. Sharks cruise below the sargassum, searching for prey. Whales crisscross the waters of the Sargasso on their yearly migrations, and depend on the rich feeding grounds they find there. Some whales, like orcas and sperm whales, hunt for fish, squid, and bigger prey. Other whales, like humpbacks and right whales, feed on plankton. When these animals eventually die, their bodies nourish all sorts of scavengers and decomposers: crabs, worms, insects, bacteria.

From top to bottom, the Sargasso Sea is brimming with life. And all of those organisms, from the tiniest shrimp to the largest whale, depend on seaweed for their existence.

WHO OWNS THE SARGASSO SEA?

Look at a globe, and you'll see that almost three-fourths of it shows blue water. The ocean covers 70 percent of the earth. But who owns the ocean?

In 1982, the United Nations organized an international treaty that was agreed to by many (but not all) of the countries in the world. This treaty established that the rights to the ocean's resources within two hundred miles of a nation's coastline are controlled by that nation, and only its citizens can harvest fish, seaweed, shellfish, or any marine life, or extract minerals, oil, or gas in that zone.

How about the rest of the ocean? Beyond the two-hundred-mile limit are millions of square miles of open ocean that are legally considered the "high seas." Hundreds of miles from land, places like the Sargasso Sea don't belong to any person, or any country. Laws protecting seaweed against overharvesting, poaching, littering, or polluting must have dozens of nations agreeing to cooperate.

There are many threats looming for the Sargasso. Plastic pollution and overfishing are two of the worst, and as oceans warm and currents change, the Sargasso is under even more stress. The people of Bermuda, the only land within the Sargasso, decided to enlist the help of other nations, and in 2010 Bermuda led the way in establishing the Sargasso Sea Alliance. This international group brings together all sorts of organizations—not-for-profits like the World Wildlife Fund and Mission Blue, universities, and governments of many nations—all committed to protecting the Sargasso and its wildlife. They do research on the Sargasso's ecosystem, and work to create international laws that can protect it. People from countries close to the Sargasso, like the Bahamas, the United States, the Azores, and Costa Rica are joined by people from more distant places like New Zealand, Canada, and the UK, because they realize that what happens in the Sargasso can impact every country on earth.

The only breeding ground for endangered eels is in the Sargasso—so no matter where you live, if you like to eat eels, the Sargasso matters to you. If you dream of seeing a whale or a shark or a sea turtle someday, the Sargasso matters to you. If you want there to be enough tuna, swordfish, and other species of fish to feed the world's hungry people, the Sargasso matters to you—and to everyone.

SEAWEED ON THE MENU

Seaweed is the basis for uncountable numbers of food chains. It's an essential link in the lives of most marine creatures. But there's another organism that we often forget is a part of nature's complex pattern: us! How does our own food chain look—and how might it change in the future?

As climate change affects our planet, the world's weather is changing in unpredictable ways. The farmers who produce our food are among the first people to feel these effects. Storms and hurricanes are worsening around the globe, sometimes causing disastrous flooding. Other regions are seared by droughts. One of the greatest challenges of the future will be to feed the world's eight billion inhabitants.

Seaweed has enormous potential as a rich source of nutrition to feed hungry people. In the century to come, you may be depending on bread baked from seaweed meal instead of wheat flour. Would you eat a sargassum salad? Or try a rockweed burger?

Seaweed may be a vital food source in the future. But eating seaweed is nothing new. Hundreds of species of seaweed have been on people's menus for a long time—a very long time. Who were the first humans bold enough to take a bite of seaweed?

FIVE
THE EDIBLE FOREST

The village on the riverbank had been abandoned for centuries. No hint remained of why the inhabitants had left their homes abruptly, leaving their goods scattered, with remnants of uneaten meals on the ground. Once, a community of families had lived here. Now only a few clues remained to help archeologists reconstruct the past.

In the 1970s, the Monte Verde historic site was excavated in the hills of Chile, in South America. Soon after the villagers had left, the river flooded, sealing the village site in mud, which kept out bacteria and rot. Diggers found amazingly well-preserved clothing, tools, cooking hearths, and even scraps of the meals the villagers had cooked, including bits of shellfish, nuts, and llama meat. But the most surprising finds, in a spot forty miles from the ocean—no small journey in ancient times—were samples of nine species of seaweed!

The archeologists discovered that some of the seaweed had

been dried into clumps and chewed like tobacco, possibly as medicine. Other bits of seaweed were found on the tips of stone knives. Leftover scraps of cooked seaweed lay near the hearthstones. Plainly, seaweed was an important part of these people's daily lives. How long ago did the villagers who munched on seaweed live there?

Scientists used a technique called carbon dating to figure out how old the site was. They discovered that those seaweed meals had been eaten by people who lived there fourteen thousand years ago! No one knows who the first person to sample seaweed was, but ten thousand years before the Egyptian pyramids were built, many Stone Age humans depended on seaweed for food and medicine.

Living so far from the coast, it wasn't easy for them to transport lots of seaweed. But even a few bites of the stuff can be a lifesaver.

A WEEDY VITAMIN PILL

A nibble of seaweed has lots of the essential vitamins and minerals humans need to keep us healthy. Many seaweeds are so rich in nutrients that today we call them superfoods. Ounce for ounce, sea lettuce has more iron than spinach does. Dulse has more protein than eggs or steak.

Kelp has more calcium than milk. And seaweeds are high in vitamins—some have more vitamin C than orange juice.

Seaweed is especially high in trace minerals. These are minerals that the human body needs to be healthy, but they're only needed in very small amounts: unfamiliar substances like iodine, molybdenum, and chromium. Nowadays we don't worry about them since it's easy to get all our trace minerals from vitamin pills or fortified foods like breakfast cereals. But before the twentieth century, it was difficult for humans, especially poor people on a limited diet, to get these life-giving nutrients. In many ancient coastal settlements, especially in Asia, seaweed eating became the norm early in prehistoric times.

You can't survive on nothing but seaweed, though. For one thing, seaweed doesn't have a lot of calories, which give you energy. But adding seaweed to their diet must have saved countless people from the effects of malnutrition and helped to protect them from disease. Because seaweed is not only good food, it's good medicine.

A DOSE OF SEAWEED

Far back in history, healers used seaweed as a cure for diseases like scurvy, rickets, and pellagra. No one knew what caused these deadly ailments, but they often afflicted poor people. It wasn't until well into the 1900s that scientists realized that these diseases were caused by a lack of the invisible, untastable chemicals that we call vitamins. Scurvy, for example, is caused by a lack of vitamin C, and could be cured in days by a dose of vitamin-rich seaweed.

Another benefit of seaweed is that it has huge amounts of a mineral called iodine. Lack of iodine leads to thyroid disease, painful neck swellings called goiters, and even death. These days, iodine is usually added to table salt. (Look at a container of salt in the grocery store—it will probably be labeled "This salt contains iodine, a necessary nutrient.") Just a nibble of salty snacks gives us abundant iodine. But since iodine is rarely found on land, it used to be very hard to come by—unless you lived near a source of seafood. Just a bite or two of seaweed could cure disease caused by iodine deficiency.

THE GAMBLER'S GRASS

For centuries, seaweed has been a part of Asian culture. Most Japanese meals include the paper-thin, salty food called nori.

Written recipes for Japanese nori date back more than a thousand years. But even long before that, it was a valued food—and not just for people facing starvation. In ancient times, baskets of delicious nori were offered to the emperor of Japan as part of seaside villagers' taxes.

Traditionally, Japanese people collected nori from the wild. But even as long ago as the 1500s, wild populations of this beloved food were running low. So "nori fishers" began growing it artificially, by stringing underwater nets on

Seaweed Close-Up: Porphyra

Porphyra is the seaweed used to make nori. The seaweed is cut up and mixed into a paste, then spread out to dry in thin sheets, in a process very much like making paper. *Porphyra* is too tough to chew raw, but toasting it brings out a nutty flavor. It's almost half protein, and filled with Omega-3 and Omega-6 fatty acids, which are very heart-healthy.

Even if you're not familiar with eating seaweed, you might have encountered nori—it's the dark-green strip that holds sushi together.

poles across quiet bays. Nori sprouted on the meshes and was harvested by pulling up the nets and slicing off the strands of seaweed. Generations of nori fishers tended their underwater farms, by boat or sometimes by walking on stilts in the deep water. It was a common sight to see nori farmers wading in the bay like long-legged birds.

But seaweed farming was a chancy business. There was no obvious method for planting nori like you'd plant other crops. There were no seeds to be scattered, no seedlings to transplant. Nori farmers would string their nets and wait, but some years the nets would be empty. They called their unreliable crop "gambler's grass," because you never knew if it would grow or not. In years when the nori mysteriously failed to appear, famine set in. The secret of how nori reproduced remained a mystery for centuries.

SEAWEED SEEDS?

The problem was that people were thinking of seaweed as a plant. But plants like corn, petunias, or soybeans have seeds. Want more corn? Plant a seed. Seaweed doesn't work like that. Remember that seaweeds aren't plants, they're algae.

Algae don't have flowers or produce fruit or seeds. Like fungi, ferns, and mosses, they create tiny seedlike particles called spores. Spores of some species of algae just drift in the water. Other spores, called zoospores, are like little animals: they have wriggling tails and actually swim!

But the spores *don't* grow directly into seaweed. Instead, they develop into a leaflike structure called a **gametophyte**. This produces male or female cells, which unite with cells from other gametophytes, creating a new seaweed. **Phycologists** (scientists who study algae) are still investigating algae's complex process of reproduction.

SEAWEED ON YOUR MENU?

For some of us, the idea of eating seaweed seems disgusting. For

Seaweed Science: Kathleen Drew-Baker

She was a scientist who loved the sea, and especially seaweed. In the early 1900s, Kathleen Drew-Baker was one of the first scientists to study marine algae at a university, and to teach classes about it. But she was fired from her job as a professor at Manchester University in England because she got married—and in 1928, married women often weren't allowed to hold jobs.

Determined to continue her research, she designed her own laboratory, complete with saltwater tanks where the water rose and fell like ocean tides. She concentrated on the mysterious *Porphyra*, which is harvested for food around the world.

Porphyra spores settle on bits of clam or oyster shell, growing into a pinkish substance that coats the shells, but for centuries no one knew what this slimy stuff was. Drew-Baker discovered that the pink mass is actually a growth stage (gametophyte) of *Porphyra*. Want to grow nori? Just make sure you have a hard surface for the spores to settle on.

Her discovery made it possible to create nori farms that produced a reliable crop. To this day she is respected in Japan as the "Mother of the Sea," and an annual festival is held in her honor.

some of us, seaweed is a tasty part of the day's usual menu. In some places, instead of buying crunchy, salty popcorn at a movie theater, you might buy crunchy, salty seaweed snacks. Many cultures around the world have used seaweed not as a last-ditch survival food

or a nasty-tasting medicine, but as a gourmet treat.

If your only experience of seaweed has been slimy, rubbery stuff that lies on the beach or brushes creepily against you while you swim, it can be hard to imagine eating it for fun. But seaweed has an incredible variety of tastes and textures. It can be crisp as corn chips, or smooth as guacamole. It can be a savory part of a stew, or a bright bit of color in a salad.

Today, more people are depending on seaweed for food. In Japan alone, grocery stores sell millions of pounds of seaweed every year. But where does all that seaweed come from?

Seaweed Close-Up: Giant Kelp
(*Macrocystis pyrifera*)

Kelp is great food for people, and essential for many species of wildlife. But giant kelp forests are under siege from an unlikely threat: tiny purple sea urchins. These small, spiky creatures are a native species that have always been a part of the kelp forest ecosystem off the coast of California. The inch-long urchins nibble on fronds of towering bull kelp a hundred feet high. But now millions upon millions of sea urchins are devouring the forest.

The kelp ecosystem got out of balance due to a marine heat wave. Until recently, starfish preyed on the sea urchins, keeping their numbers in check. But climate change brings rising temperatures. The warmer seawater encouraged the spread of a wasting disease that killed most of the starfish. Sea otters also eat urchins, and the decrease in the sea otter population has contributed to the boom of urchins. With its natural predators gone, the urchin population surged out of control, destroying the kelp.

Volunteer groups of divers are picking urchins off the kelp by hand. They're hoping to slow the decline until scientists can find a remedy. But more research is needed to find ways to keep the urchins in check, at a level that can let the wild forest sustain itself.

OVERHARVESTING

The vast oceans of the world seem limitless, as if there's no end to their abundance. But as fisheries collapse and species become endangered, we're beginning to learn that there's a limit to the sea's bounty. Just as we shouldn't cut down every tree in a forest, or catch every last fish, we need to be aware of the dangers of overharvesting seaweed.

When a rain forest burns or an old-growth forest is clear-cut, we can see horrifying pictures of the environmental damage: eroded soil, burned trees, rotting stumps. But seaweed spends

Seaweed Close-Up: Limu Kala (Sargassum echinocarpum)

In many languages of the South Seas, the word *limu* means *seaweed*. In ancient Hawaii, seaweed was a prized food, and it still is today. Dozens of types are grown in seaweed gardens. A species known as *limu kala* is used for medicine, especially to soothe cuts caused by sharp coral. It can be used to soothe angry feelings, too.

Limu kala is part of a traditional ceremony of reconciliation. Family members who have quarreled might show their forgiveness by eating tender leaves of limu kala. Sometimes leis (necklaces made of flowers) include limu kala as a sign of peace and harmony.

most of its life hidden underwater, so it's easy to miss signs of critical deforestation—until it's too late.

For example, rockweed has been harvested for centuries, for food, fertilizer, or livestock feed. But in the twenty-first century, rockweed is in ever more demand. The old-time tradition of people cutting rockweed by hand didn't make a huge difference to the vast seaweed forests that line the North Atlantic coasts. But modern flat-bottomed barges carrying mechanical harvesting machines can slice millions of pounds of rockweed off the sea bottom like a combine clear-cutting a field of wheat.

There need to be more regulations about how much seaweed is harvested, just like there are laws about hunting deer or catching fish. Seaweed harvested from the wild is unprotected by law in some nations. Other countries, including the United States, are just beginning to decide on laws about how much seaweed can be taken. We don't want to harvest so much of this wonderful resource that it goes extinct just as we're finding out how valuable it is.

So how to provide seaweed for potentially billions of people to use without destroying the environment? Well, if there can be a seaweed forest, why not a seaweed farm?

Imagine a farmer who drives a boat instead of a tractor. Imagine seeds that can swim. Crops you never have to water, with fertilizer delivered for free. Imagine whole fields of delicious and nutritious crops . . . completely underwater.

SIX
FARMING THE FOREST

Ever since those first nori fishers wading on stilts, people have been inventing ways to make seaweed grow when and where they wanted it. For centuries, most seaweed farming has been done by Asian nations like Japan, Korea, and China, and today most seaweed eaten in the USA comes from Asia. But there's a growing "green wave" of seaweed farms along both the east and west coasts of North America and in many other nations as well.

AQUACULTURE VERSUS AGRICULTURE

Aquaculture, which is farming in the water, is often easier on the environment than land farming. It can be a sustainable way to use the ocean's resources, using the seas' wealth to meet our needs without destroying the very resources we need so desperately.

Farms near coastal areas are especially at risk from erosion, sea-level rise, and flooding. Many areas—California, for example—are hard-hit by drought and wildfires. It's estimated that rising temperatures and drought will affect many California crops, making it harder to grow foods like almonds, grapes, oranges, avocados, and walnuts. All over the world, climate change is affecting the world's farms in unpredictable ways.

But seaweed aquaculture doesn't use up scarce water resources, because of course you don't need to water your underwater crop. And there's no need to drive a tractor across the field dispensing chemical fertilizers that are a major cause of water pollution. Nutrition is delivered free of charge by ocean currents.

Around the world, fish populations are at dangerously low levels due to overfishing. Commercial fisheries are collapsing—which means that people who make their living from the sea are

facing hard times. Seaweed farming can provide jobs and income to places that used to depend on fishing.

But it's not only humans that benefit when large areas of seaweed are nurtured.

A land farmer growing corn doesn't want wildlife hanging out in the cornfield—deer nibbling his crop, raccoons stealing ears. But planting seaweed can be a win-win for both humans and wildlife. Fish, especially young ones, use the underwater gardens for food and shelter. And it's much more than just fish—oysters, mussels, shrimp, eels, seals, otters, crabs . . . a whole ecosystem can thrive within a seaweed farm.

And growing seaweed can help heal the damaged ocean. As levels of carbon dioxide in the air increase from human activity such as burning **fossil fuels**, the amount absorbed by the ocean also increases. When too much CO_2 is absorbed by seawater, a series of chemical reactions occur, making the water more acid. This acidification is harmful to marine life, including fish and shellfish, and acidification is a major destroyer of coral reefs. But seaweed sucks CO_2 out of the water, improving water quality and lowering acid levels.

HOW TO BECOME A SEAWEED FARMER

Imagine you've decided to become a seaweed famer. First, you need a farm. On land, a farmer must own hundreds or even thousands of acres to plant enough crops or feed enough cows to make a profit. But a seaweed farmer only needs a small slice of sea.

In the United States, as in many countries, you don't buy water like you buy land. The ocean and the sea bottom within two

hundred miles of the coast are regulated by the government, and you pay for the right to use a particular area of seawater for your farm. (Each state has different regulations about aquaculture.) Many farmers lease only a few dozen acres each year.

There are lots of different ways to design a seaweed farm. Let's consider one possible way to farm the cold, deep waters of the North Atlantic.

You'll only need a small area of ocean, because seaweed farming can be vertical. On land, a field of corn stretches out to the horizon. Your underwater farm will reach from the surface to the bottom. Just as in the days of the original nori farms, the idea is to provide a surface that seaweed can attach to. Thin ropes are anchored to the bottom and held up by floating buoys. Now the farming is ready to begin.

But where to get seaweed "seeds" to plant? Say you want to grow kelp, a highly nutritious alga that's famous for fast growth. You first collect some kelp fronds that are fertile and ready to give off spores. If you're just starting out, you might buy these from a nursery, or get them from the wild. You only need a very small amount, leaving plenty of wild kelp.

You sow your seaweed not in the open ocean, but in a small tank of seawater. Gently slicing open a frond of kelp, you release the spores into an aquarium chilled to the proper temperature. Each spore is too small to see without a microscope, but when you cut into the kelp frond you'll see the aquarium turn brownish as a cloud of spores fills the water. The spores need a surface to settle on—in the wild, they'd use a rock or a bit of shell, but in your aquarium they land on lengths of string wrapped around a row of plastic pipes.

In a few days, you'll have some baby seaweeds. Let them grow until they're about one-sixteenth of an inch long—the string will look like it's a bit furry. Then it's time to "outplant" the weedlets by boating or scuba diving out to your seaweed farm and attaching the weedy strings to the ropes in the open ocean. Then you wait, checking on the farm every few days to be sure everything is still in place.

Winds and rough weather can threaten the crop, washing away ropes and buoys. But if all goes well, your seaweed crop is ready to begin harvesting in just a few weeks. Haul up the ropes and cut off the tender young kelp that's sprouting all along the lines. Put the ropes back in the water, and kelp will keep growing for many months.

Just as not all places on land are the same, not all areas of water are the same. On land, you might have dry hills or damp lowlands, or areas of richer or poorer soil. In the sea there are differences,

too. Near the surface there is more sunlight and warmth; farther down it's darker and colder. And just as wind sweeps over the land, currents sweep through the water, carrying loads of nutrients at different depths. A good seaweed farmer analyzes the patterns of seawater like a land farmer studies the soil.

For seaweed to be a reliable resource for potentially billions of people, we'll be needing a lot of it! Can we grow enough seaweed along coastal regions, or could we site huge seaweed farms far out to sea? It might be possible to design massive farms, far from land, able to withstand storms and hurricanes. But where would the farmers live? Could seaweed farms be mostly automated, monitored by drones? Could they be deep enough underwater that storms would pass over them? Seaweed farmers are just starting to explore these possibilities.

THE PERFECT FOOD?

The reason seaweed is so fast-growing and rich in nutrients is that it soaks up minerals from the seawater that surrounds it. But seaweed can also soak up some things we don't want to eat.

Land plants that are grown in polluted soil can absorb pollutants into their tissues. In the same way, if seaweed grows in polluted water, it can absorb harmful chemicals, including the substances known as heavy metals.

They're called "heavy" not because they're heavy like a ton

of bricks, but because of their density and chemical structure. Heavy metals can be toxic even in small amounts. Arsenic, cadmium, lead, and mercury are all heavy metals that can be found in seaweeds grown in polluted waters, especially near factories, ports, and the outflow of polluted rivers.

In 2011, a tsunami hit Japan's Fukushima nuclear power plant, which released radioactive toxins into the ocean. Seaweed crops as far away as the coast of California soaked up some of the radioactivity. The government of Japan banned the sale or export of many kinds of foods affected by the Fukushima disaster, including seaweed, for a long time. The US Food and Drug Administration continues to monitor seaweed products for toxins from Fukushima.

Seaweed farmers need to be sure that the water they grow seaweed in does not have high amounts of pollution. The cold waters around the coasts of Norway, Iceland, and Canada are some of the cleanest in the ocean, and seaweed farms are common in these areas. In the United States, seaweed farms are booming in New England, Alaska, and the Pacific Northwest.

But in many countries, including the United States, seaweed is such a new and unusual food source that as yet there are few laws controlling it. Research is needed to develop more precise ways to measure toxins in seaweed to make sure the seaweed we buy is safe to eat, just as the federal government monitors fruit, vegetables, and meat we buy in the grocery store.

And just as in the past, seaweed will be medicine as well as food. Healers of long ago found that seaweed helped combat ailments like scurvy and goiters. Now researchers are finding promising ways that the chemicals naturally found in seaweed can fight heart disease, diabetes, and cancer.

What we eat has a big effect on how healthy we are. Doctors have long known that fruits and vegetables are healthy foods—and now it turns out that "sea vegetables" are among the healthiest things we can eat. Not only do they have all those great vitamins and minerals, but they're loaded with chemical compounds called antioxidants, which can help lower the risk of many serious illnesses, including heart disease and cancer.

Seaweed can't miraculously cure every disease. But research is just beginning to show that compounds derived from certain seaweeds, especially red algae like Irish moss, may offer strong defenses against many ailments. They may slow the growth of cancer cells. They may slow the degeneration of brain function that causes Alzheimer's disease. They may help the body regulate blood sugar levels to control diabetes. But as yet no one knows where this research will lead.

So seaweed can help us fight disease. It can nourish hungry people. It's salty as bacon, crunchy as potato chips, filled with vitamins, and it's low-fat, too! For sure, seaweed will be on your plate in the future—and you might learn to love it.

And it's not just humans who find seaweed tasty. You know who really likes to pig out on seaweed? Pigs. Sheep. Chickens. Horses. Goats. And a billion hungry cows.

SEVEN
CLEANING THE AIR

Ginger is a picky eater. She's quite choosy about how her food looks and smells, and she hates to try new foods. She loves apples, molasses, corn, and hay, but she's not too sure about seaweed.

Ginger is a cow, part of a furry, four-legged team made up of a dozen black-and-white Holsteins, and they're in charge of taste-testing different types of animal feed. They're helping University of California researchers find out what flavors of seaweed cows like to eat. After Ginger and the other cows sample a new recipe, the researchers lead them to a stall that's set up with a machine that can analyze chemicals in their breath. The cows burp into the machine, which reveals that eating seaweed is lowering the amount of a gas called **methane** in their digestive systems.

And that discovery could help to change the world—not just for gassy cows and dairy farmers, for everyone.

Why should we care if cows burp a bit? Because methane is a

powerful **greenhouse gas**. Greenhouse gases are gases in Earth's atmosphere that allow the sun's heat and light to pass through them, but they don't let the heat back out again. They trap the sun's heat, holding it near the earth's surface and raising the planet's temperature. Carbon dioxide is the greenhouse gas we hear about the most, but methane is even more efficient at trapping heat.

And a major cause of methane production is digestive gas from livestock. You might think, Oh well, how much air pollution can a few cow burps cause? Animals like cows, pigs, and sheep produce more methane in the United States than planes, trucks, and cars combined. Some scientists estimate that livestock produce up to 20 percent of all greenhouse gases worldwide. Most of that is caused by cattle.

In the United States there are almost one hundred million cows—that's about one for every three people. Worldwide there are more than a billion of them.

This massive population explosion of cows is having a massive effect on our planet. Enormous "factory farms" cram cattle together in small pens called feedlots, where they're fed corn and other grains that will quickly fatten them up. Many of these cattle end up as inexpensive fast-food hamburgers. Raising food for all these cows takes huge amounts of water and fertilizer, and an incredible amount of land. In the United States (not counting Alaska), a whopping 40 percent of the nation's land is used for pasture for cows or raising feed for cows.

To most of us, a cheeseburger tastes really, really good. Beef has long been one of the most basic foods in the USA, and now its popularity is rising all over the world. Unfortunately for cheeseburger fans, one of the best ways to fight climate change is by lowering our consumption of beef. But realistically, meat and dairy products are going to be a big part of the world's diet. We need to learn to raise farm animals in ways that are sustainable for the planet.

But how?

ASKING A QUESTION

The solution to a problem often begins with asking a simple question. Ginger's taste-testing research project goes back to when Canadian farmer Joe Dorgan tried to solve the mystery of why seaweed was so good for his cows.

Dr. Kinley began the investigation with Joe's beloved Irish moss.

He analyzed the digestive fluid from the stomach of a cow that had been eating Irish moss, and discovered that it had far less methane than usual.

This was the answer to the riddle. It wasn't just the extra blast of vitamins and minerals that was making the cows healthier. Seaweed was helping the animals' stomachs to work more efficiently. Methane gas is given off when food is not well digested. A lot of the energy that the food could provide was leaving the cow's body uselessly (and stinkily). Cow farts contain a small amount of methane, but about 95 percent of it comes out as burps.

Adding Irish moss to the diet made the animal's whole digestive system run more smoothly, like oiling a machine. This gave the animal more energy to spare for other things. That's why Joe Dorgan's seaweed-fed cows were giving more milk, growing more muscle, and giving birth to more calves. Dr. Kinley's chemical analysis showed that the seaweed additive reduced cows' methane-filled burps by 20 percent.

SUPER SEAWEED?

Dr. Kinley was excited by the possibilities of Irish moss as a way to fight climate change. But then he began to wonder: Among all the thousands of species of seaweeds in the ocean, was there one that could work even better?

"That's when I started the global search that brought me to Australia looking for that super seaweed," he says. He set up a laboratory in his native Australia—an island nation surrounded by seaweed. After testing dozens of species, he tried a type of red algae. It's called red sea plume, but the scientific name for it is *Asparagopsis taxiformis.*

It's a beautiful seaweed, deep red like Irish moss, but larger, with graceful branching fronds. *Asparagopsis* reaches up to the sun like an underwater tree, swaying back and forth in the warm, wave-tossed waters near coral reefs. And when Dr. Kinley tested *Asparagopsis*, the results were astounding.

"In the laboratory it was a bit of a shocker when I first found it," he remembers, "because I thought the instruments weren't working properly because I couldn't find methane at all. It was reducing methane below the detection limits of the instruments we were using. I had never seen that before."

Asparagopsis, he found, works even better than Irish moss—and you need less of it! In some cases, he found that adding

Seaweed Science: Inside a Cow's Stomach

Cows and other grazing animals eat plant foods like grass, ground-up corn cobs, and grain. These foods are made of cells with sturdy walls of fibers called cellulose, which build strong grass stems and corn stalks. But they're difficult foods to digest.

Cows' stomachs (like yours) contain millions of microscopic bacteria, which help break down the food they eat into tiny particles. But unlike humans, cows have a lot of a special kind of bacteria called *methanogens* in their stomachs. These powerful little specks can dissolve tough cells of cellulose into nutrients that the cow can use for energy. That's why cows can eat grass and we can't.

But during the breaking-down process, these microbes give off carbon and hydrogen molecules, which combine to form methane (CH_4). Methane is a gas, which the cow has to get rid of, from one end or the other.

Irish moss, like most seaweeds, contains a substance called bromoform ($CHBr_3$). It's a kind of natural antibiotic, which helps to protect the algae from bacteria. Adding seaweed to the cows' food fights bacteria—including the methanogens. The bromoform slows the methanogens down and disrupts their activity—fortunately, *after* they've broken down the tough cellulose but *before* they create methane.

Seaweed Close-Up: Red Sea Plume
(*Asparagopsis taxiformis*)

This feathery seaweed grows in warm tropical waters around the world. In Hawaiian it's called *limu kohu*, or "pleasing seaweed," because it's so delicious. For many centuries it's been part of a traditional Hawaii dish called *poke*, which is made of raw fish and coconut milk covered with sprinkles of this seaweed.

even a tiny amount, making up only 2 percent of a cow's diet, can eliminate up to 98 percent of methane emissions.

NOW WHAT?

It would seem as though the seaweed-loving cows of Prince Edward Island have led us to the solution for one of the causes of climate change. Yay, problem solved!

Or is it? The problems of climate change are bewildering and complex. The warming of our planet is the result of many complicated factors, all interwoven and affecting each other. There are no quick and easy solutions.

The first challenge in using seaweed to lower methane is persuading cows to eat the stuff. Ever hear the old expression "You can lead a horse to water but you can't make him drink"? You can feed your cows seaweed, but you can't make them eat it—unless they like the taste.

Cows evolved as grazing animals, and in the wild there might be plants that could be harmful. So cows are instinctively very cautious about trying new tastes. Joe Dorgan's cows on Prince Edward Island were used to nibbling fishy-tasting seaweed. But some cows won't touch it.

That's why researchers are trying to find out which seaweeds not only work best for methane reduction but are also practical for use on farms. Ginger and the other cows in the research project were given a variety of seaweeds to try. At first the fussy cows rejected them all, but fortunately cows seem to have a sweet tooth. Researchers tried many different ingredients to flavor the seaweed, including curry powder, but found that a sticky mixture of molasses worked best. Seaweed-molasses pudding might not sound delicious to you, but Ginger loves it.

But other challenges lie ahead. *Asparagopsis* is not a very common seaweed, and it's hard to gather; it grows only in shallow water that's tossed and swirled by waves. Most of the samples Dr. Kinley used were handpicked by divers off the coast of Australia and New Zealand. But in order to really make a dent in methane, huge amounts will be needed—after all, we're talking about a billion cows.

So *Asparagopsis* will have to be grown by seaweed farmers. Experiments on ways to grow *Asparagopsis* in large amounts are just beginning. The challenge is to invent a feed additive that is tasty (to cows), affordable, and easily available to farmers all

over the world. Developing environmentally sustainable sources of seaweed will be one of the major challenges of the twenty-first century.

But there is enormous potential in this solution that began with a curious farmer asking, Why? And who knows what other solutions seaweed forests might offer us in the future?

EIGHT
THE ONCE AND FUTURE SEAWEED

For thousands of years, the Indigenous people of the Shinnecock Nation have lived with the waters of Shinnecock Bay, on the south shore of Long Island in New York state. They fished, gathered shell-fish, and harvested seaweed for food. But in recent years, the bay has changed. It's no longer a stretch of sparkling water rich with wildlife. Increased development on Long Island—more houses, shopping malls, golf courses—is polluting the water.

Fertilizer used on land runs off into the bay when it rains. The fertilizer isn't toxic—it's just that it's packed with nutrients, especially nitrogen. And as we've seen before, too many nutrients equals too much seaweed. Massive blooms of algae clog the clear water of the bay. When the algae rots, the process of decomposition uses up oxygen, lowering the water quality and killing fish and shellfish.

Six Shinnecock women have decided to do something about it. "We have got to do more to help Mother Earth and cleanse her waters and honor her in a better way," says Becky Genia, a member of the Shinnecock Nation. With support from the Sisters of

Saint Joseph and a not-for-profit organization called GreenWave, she and the other women are launching a kelp farm. Seaweed's superpower of absorbing chemicals from water makes it an effective way to filter pollutants from harbors, rivers, and bays. Kelp, one of the fastest-growing seaweeds, excels at soaking up pollutants, especially nitrogen.

This technique of growing seaweeds to filter pollution from water is being used all over the world: to clean up oil spills in

Alaska, to soak up sewage polluting Sydney Harbor in Australia, and in many other places. With all these projects, the goal is to restore nature's balance: clean water with not too many nutrients, but enough so that seaweed can flourish. Then seaweed can do what it does best—be the strong foundation for a healthy ocean ecosystem.

SEAWEED IN THE GAS TANK?

Perhaps someday you'll drive up to the pump and fuel your car with seaweed. Chemists are researching the use of seaweed as **biofuel**: fuel made from living plants or algae, as opposed to fossil

fuels like oil or coal. Ethanol made from corn is the most commonly used biofuel today, and is often added to gasoline. (Next time your car is gassed up, check the pump to see if it includes ethanol.) As we've seen, however, growing corn uses up land, requires large amounts of pesticides and chemical fertilizers, and guzzles scarce water resources.

One of the most tantalizing possibilities for seaweed is its use as a fuel. Could we stop using fossil fuels for cars, trucks, and airplanes? Could seaweed someday power the world?

It's not impossible. Seaweed can be dried, ground up, and broken down into an oil that can be used as fuel—it's already been used successfully to fuel cars, and was even tested on an aircraft carrier! But worldwide, humans use tens of millions of barrels of oil a day. There are tremendous challenges to producing enough seaweed fuel to make a real dent in climate change.

Millions, perhaps billions, of tons of seaweed would have to be grown. And it takes energy to harvest all that seaweed, and to process it into usable oil. Many companies that were researching biofuels have given up because the process is too expensive, but some are still investigating the possibilities. The problems are big, but the rewards could be huge.

THE BEGINNING

Seaweed has always been the basis of ocean ecosystems. It's been used by humans for millennia, and it's now on the cutting edge of science. Seaweed is turning out to be a game changer in so many unexpected ways.

Imagine what the future might hold. Biodegradable plastic

made from seaweed. Cars fueled with seaweed. You might drink clean, safe water filtered by seaweed. Maybe you'll live in a house roofed with insulation of compressed seaweed, or wear clothing made of seaweed fabric. Someday this book might be printed on paper made from seaweed. There's no end to the possibilities.

Seaweed can feed us. It can heal us. It cradles wildlife, cleans water, and creates the very air we breathe. And now we know that seaweed can help in the fight to save our planet. The world's vast and weighty problems can seem unsolvable, but the answers to catastrophe aren't completely out of reach. There's hope for the future, after all.

It's lying there on the sand, right under our flip-flops.

GLOSSARY

algae (singular alga): Plantlike living things that make their own food from sunlight. Most seaweeds are algae.

algin: A jellylike substance found inside some seaweeds that absorbs water, keeping the seaweed moist when it's exposed to the air.

aquaculture: Farming that occurs underwater, producing seaweed, fish, shellfish, or other foods.

autotroph: A living thing that can make its own food, usually by photosynthesis.

biofuel: Fuel made from plants or algae that were living recently, used as a substitute for fossil fuel made from organisms that died millions of years ago.

climate change: A significant change in weather patterns over a period of years.

deforestation: Destruction of a forest ecosystem, on land or in the sea.

fossil fuel: A fuel formed in the earth eons ago from the remains of ancient plants and animals.

frond: A leaflike structure, part of a plant or an alga.

gametophyte: One of two phases in the reproductive cycle of nonflowering plants and algae.

greenhouse gas: A gas that traps the sun's heat close to the earth.

holdfast: A rootlike structure that anchors seaweeds and other organisms to a surface.

krill: Tiny shrimplike creatures that float in the oceans as part of plankton.

methane: A greenhouse gas. Methane can be given off when something that was once alive, like plants or animals, decomposes or is digested.

methanogen: A methane-producing bacterium.

nutrient: A substance used by a living thing to survive and grow.

photic zone: The uppermost layer of water where sunlight can penetrate, and plants and algae can grow.

photosynthesis: The process by which green plants and algae manufacture their own food using carbon dioxide, water, and light from the sun.

phycologist: A scientist who studies algae.

phytoplankton: Tiny organisms that drift in water and photosynthesize to make their own food.

upwelling: The rising of cool, dense water toward the ocean surface, usually carrying nutrients with it.

FOOD FROM THE FOREST

Maybe you've already enjoyed tasty seaweed treats. But if seaweed snacking is new to you, you might want to ease into it by adding seaweed to foods you usually eat. Think of it as sprinkling tasty vitamins on your food. Seaweed adds a salty tang to salads, coleslaw, or sandwiches. You can also buy prepackaged seaweed snacks, crisp and salty like potato chips.

Seaweed is an especially good choice for vegetarians and vegans, as it's even higher than meat in vitamin B_{12} and protein. Sometimes seaweed is marketed as "sea vegetables"–sounds tastier!

MERMAID CONFETTI

*With the help of an adult, try this recipe for tasty drop biscuits
with seaweed bits.*

⅓ cup shortening

1¾ cups flour (whole-wheat pastry flour is great)

2½ teaspoons baking powder

¾ teaspoon salt

1 cup milk (approximately)

1 package dried seaweed snacks

Preheat oven to 450 degrees.

Mix shortening, flour, baking powder, and salt. Stir in milk till dough is a sticky ball.

Crumble dried seaweed snacks into bits. Mix into the dough.

Drop dough by spoonfuls onto a greased cookie sheet.

Bake until golden brown, 10 to 12 minutes.

SEAWEED INSIDE AND OUT

Seaweed is good for your insides, but it's also good for your outsides. Adding seaweed to bathwater is great for your skin. You can buy commercially made seaweed bath salts, or just toss some seaweed, dried or fresh, into a tubful of hot water. Dive in! Some of the nutrients in the algae will ooze out into the water and be absorbed by your skin. Seaweed can help your skin glow with health, and can be very soothing to irritated skin.

The nutrients in seaweed are good for any living things that need vitamins and minerals, including your dog! Or your cat, or turtle, or hamster. Some pet food manufacturers are now adding seaweed to pet food. High in nutrition and easily digested, it's helpful for pets with sensitive stomachs, allergies, or health issues. Guinea pigs especially need vitamin C—a pinch of seaweed added to their food can make for a healthy pig.

Even plants love seaweed! You can add it to your garden as a rich fertilizer. Add seaweed to the compost bin, use it as mulch around plants, or shovel it straight into the soil, as Joe Dorgan's ancestors did for so many generations. Before adding it to the garden, rinse off the salt with fresh water, as too much salt can harm plants.

Even your houseplants can enjoy a sprinkle of seaweed. Soak dried seaweed in water and water your plants with a little "seaweed tea."

FORAGING

If you live near the ocean, you can gather seaweed for yourself. But be a good caretaker of the environment as you forage.

—Don't take large amounts of seaweed. A good rule of thumb is that if you can see ten, pick one.

—Never rip seaweed from rocks, since it can't regrow. Cut a bit off the end of the seaweed, leaving the holdfasts in place, so the seaweed can regenerate from the tips.

—Spread your collecting around—a little here, a little there. Remember, every seaweed is a habitat for some creature.

—Be aware that seaweed can absorb pollutants from water. Avoid gathering seaweed from areas near buildings, factories, or pipes. Also

avoid seaweed growing in stagnant (unmoving) water. Look for seaweed that is washed by the ocean waves.

—Remember, seaweed is a nutrient powerhouse, so a little goes a long way.

—If you're going to try eating the seaweed, check with an adult, and be sure of your identification. As with any new food, sample just a small amount at first.

SEAWEED TIMELINE

Life began in the oceans. For billions of years there was no life on land at all.

Scientists debate exactly when different life forms first appeared on the planet. Hard things like dinosaur bones fossilize easily, so it's easier to establish dates for them. Soft things like seaweeds only rarely form fossils, making it harder to fit them into the fossil record.

But, give or take a few million years, this is how life on our planet likely developed.

4.5 billion years ago—Formation of planet Earth

3.7 billion—Phytoplankton—single-celled cyanobacteria—develop in the ocean

1.6 billion—Single-celled algae evolve

1 billion—Macroalgae (seaweeds that have more than one cell) develop

530 million—First fish

500 million—First land plants

450 million—Sharks

410 million—Ferns

350 million—Trees

250 million—First dinosaurs

230 million—Sea turtles

200 million—Brown algae evolve

150 million—First birds appear

81 million—*Tyrannosaurus rex*

65 million—Dinosaurs go extinct

50 million—Whales evolve

40 million—Sargassum evolves from species of seaweed that attach to the sea bottom

5-7 million—Humans evolve

12,000 BCE—People living at Monte Verde use seaweed for food and possibly medicine

2700 BCE—First Egyptian pyramids built

563 CE—St. Columba writes poem about gathering seaweed on the Irish coast

800s—First written nori recipes, records of nori used for tax paid to Japanese emperor

1400s—Europeans sail the Sargasso Sea for the first time

1500s—Early nori farms

1930s—Kathleen Drew-Baker studies seaweed reproduction

2007—Joe Dorgan and Robert Kinley start researching seaweed

2021—The Shinnecock Kelp Farmers launch their kelp farm on Long Island, NY

The future—Countless seaweed innovations waiting to be made!

WHERE TO SEE SEAWEED

*If you live near the ocean, seaweed is probably a familiar sight.
But even if you live far from the sea, you can spot algae
in many places.*

Many cities have a zoo or aquarium where you can see marine life, including seaweed. Another place to get a look at live seaweed is in a pet store. Owners of saltwater fish tanks often buy seaweed, because of course seaweed is part of their fishes' natural habitat, providing food, shelter, oxygen, and clean water.

Algae grows in fresh water, too. Most freshwater algae doesn't have holdfasts, so it often grows in still water. Look for it as a green floating mass in lakes, ponds, and even puddles. If you touch it, it might feel slimy. The slime is the algae's way of keeping moist even when the water dries up.

Like seaweed, freshwater algae can be a crucial part of an aquatic habitat. But, as in the ocean, HABs (harmful algal blooms) can be caused by too many nutrients in the water, for example if there is fertilizer runoff from farms or lawns.

If you see a film of green on a puddle, or a swirl of pondweed or lakeweed, remember you're looking at seaweed's relatives, some of Earth's most ancient forms of life.

WAYS TO HELP SEAWEED FORESTS THRIVE

When rain comes from the sky, it's the ocean touching you.

When you breathe air, it's the ocean touching you.

—Dr. Sylvia Earle, marine biologist

You may live far from the ocean and its seaweed forests, but they still affect you—and you affect seaweed, too.

Help keep plastic out of seaweed forests.

—Pick up litter.

—Avoid the use of plastic, and especially avoid single-use plastic: things that get used once and thrown away, like plastic bags and spoons.

Then think bigger.

—Can you organize a school litter pickup along a beach or riverside? (River litter washes into the ocean sooner or later.)

—What's your town's policy on plastic? Some places are starting to ban the use of plastic bags in stores. Support local laws in your town that ban single-use plastic.

Become an ocean activist.

—Write a letter to your local newspaper about a water quality issue in your neighborhood.

—Vote! Encourage everyone in your family to vote for candidates who support policies that protect the oceans and the environment. Register to vote as soon as you are old enough.

—Support nonprofits that work to protect the oceans. Mission Blue, Operation Crayweed, and the World Wildlife Fund are just a few of the excellent organizations that need support. Consider becoming a member.

—Fund-raise to help plant an underwater forest.

BIBLIOGRAPHY

WEBSITES

Augustin, Johan. "In Race for a Sustainable Alternative to Plastic, Indonesia Bets on Seaweed." Mongabay, March 25, 2020. https://news.mongabay.com/2020/03/in-race-for-a-sustainable-alternative-to-plastic-indonesia-bets-on-seaweed/.

Barth, Brian. "The Seafaring Draft Horses of Prince Edward Island." *Modern Farmer*, Dec. 16, 2015. https://modernfarmer.com/2015/12/draft-horses-harvesting-seaweed/.

C2 Montréal. "Dr. Sylvia Earle on Why Saving Our Oceans Means Saving Ourselves." January 9, 2019. https://www.c2montreal.com/post/dr-sylvia-earle-why-saving-our-oceans/#/.

California Climate and Agriculture Network. "Climate Threats to Agriculture." Modified December 7, 2021. https://calclimateag.org/climatethreatstoag/.

Canadian Press. "P.E.I. Dairy Farmer Discovers a Seaweed Diet Dramatically Cuts Cows' Methane Output." *Canadian Grocer*, Dec. 11, 2016. https://canadiangrocer.com/pei-dairy-farmer-discovers-seaweed-diet-dramatically-cuts-cows-methane-output.

Cherry, Paul, Cathal O'Hara, Pamela J. Magee, Emeir M. McSorley, and Philip J. Allsopp, "Risks and Benefits of Consuming Edible Seaweeds." *Nutrition Reviews* 77(5), 307–329. March 6, 2019. https://doi.org/10.1093/nutrit/nuy066.

Flavin, Katie, Nick Flavin, and Bill Flahive. *Kelp Farming Manual: A Guide to the Processes, Techniques, and Equipment for Farming Kelp in New England Waters*. Ocean Approved, 2013. Maine Aquaculture Association website. https://maineaqua.org/wp-content/uploads /2020/06/OceanApproved_KelpManualLowRez.pdf.

Fondriest Environmental. "Algae, Phytoplankton and Chlorophyll." Oct. 22, 2014. https://www.fondriest.com/environmentalmeasurements /parameters/water-quality/algae-phytoplanktonchlorophyll/#al gae2.

GreenWave. "Breathing Life Back into Our Planet." Accessed January 20, 2022. https://www.greenwave.org.

Harrington, Mark. "Shinnecock Women Launch Kelp Hatchery, Cultivation Operation." *Newsday*, updated August 21, 2021. https:// www.newsday.com/long-island/suffolk/shinnecock-nation-kelp -greenwave-sisters-of-st-joseph-1.50339691.

Katz, Brigit. "A Remote Scottish Island Needs Help Protecting Its Seaweed-Eating Sheep." *Smithsonian Magazine*, June 27, 2019. https://www .smithsonianmag.com/smart-news/remote-scottish-island -needs-help-protecting-its-seaweed-eating-sheep-180972496/.

Merrill, Dave, and Lauren Leatherby. "Here's How America Uses Its Land." Bloomberg, July 31, 2018. https://www.bloomberg.com /graphics/2018-us-land-use/.

NOAA. "Ocean Exploration and Research: What is Upwelling?" Modified September 29, 2020. oceanexplorer.noaa.gov/facts/upwelling .html.

North Atlantic Organics. "Atlantic-Gro Organic Sea Plant Products." June 27, 2012. www.naorganics.com/index.asp.

Operation Crayweed. "Restoring Sydney's Underwater Forests." Accessed April 9, 2021. www.operationcrayweed.com.

Pickett, Mallory, and Bob Berwyn. "In the Pacific, Global Warming Disrupted the Ecological Dance." Inside Climate News. March 16, 2021. https://insideclimatenews.org/news/16032021/pacific-ocean-climate-change-kelp-urchin-sea-otter-sea-stars/.

Roman, Joe, and James J. McCarthy. "The Whale Pump: Marine Mammals Enhance Primary Productivity in a Coastal Basin." PLoS ONE 5(10): e13255. October 11, 2010. https://doi.org/10.1371/journal.pone.0013255.

Ross, Shane. "P.E.I. Farmer Assists in Near-Eradication of Methane from Cow Farts." *CBC News*, November 18, 2016. https://www.cbc.ca/news/canada/prince-edward-island/pei-cow-farting-1.3856202.

Sargasso Sea Alliance. "The Protection and Management of the Sargasso Sea: . . . Summary Science and Supporting Evidence Case." Accessed January 4, 2021. http://www.sargassoseacommission.org/storage/documents/Sargasso.Report.9.12.pdf.

ScienceDaily. "New Health Benefits of Red Seaweeds Unveiled." Science News, June 14, 2021. https://www.sciencedaily.com/releases/2021/06/210614185554.htm.

ScienceDaily. "One-Billion-Year-Old Seaweed Fossils Identified."

Science News, February 24, 2020. https://www.sciencedaily.com /releases/2020/02/200224111339.htm.

Woods Hole Oceanographic Institution. "Phytoplankton." February 6, 2019. https://www.whoi.edu/know-your-ocean/ocean-topics /ocean-life/phytoplankton/.

BOOKS

Earle, Sylvia. *Blue Hope: Exploring and Caring for Earth's Magnificent Ocean.* Washington, DC: National Geographic, 2014.

———. *The World Is Blue: How Our Fate and the Ocean's Are One.* Washington, DC: National Geographic, 2009.

———, and Linda Glover. *Ocean: An Illustrated Atlas.* Washington, DC: National Geographic, 2009.

Hawken, Paul, ed. *Drawdown: The Most Comprehensive Plan Ever Proposed to Reverse Global Warming.* NY: Penguin Random House, 2017.

Kassinger, Ruth. *Slime: How Algae Created Us, Plague Us and Just Might Save Us.* Boston, MA: Houghton Mifflin Harcourt, 2019.

Mouritsen, Ole G. *Seaweeds: Edible, Available, and Sustainable.* Chicago: University of Chicago Press, 2013.

Smith, Bren. *Eat Like a Fish: My Adventures as a Fisherman Turned Restorative Ocean Farmer.* NY: Vintage Books, 2020.

SOURCE NOTES

CHAPTER ONE

p. 6. "All my life . . . it's good for everything." Barth, "Seafaring Draft Horses."

p. 7. "There's a mixture . . . that's what they done their business with." Ross, "PEI Farmer."

CHAPTER SEVEN

p. 62. "That's when I started . . . that super seaweed." Canadian Press, "P.E.I. Dairy Farmer."

p. 63. "In the laboratory . . . never seen that before." Canadian Press, "P.E.I. Dairy Farmer."

CHAPTER EIGHT

p. 68. "We have got to do more . . . honor her in a better way." Harrington, "Shinnecock Women."

WAYS TO HELP SEAWEED FORESTS THRIVE

p. 84. "When rain comes . . . When you breathe air, it's the ocean touching you." C2 Montréal, "Dr. Sylvia Earle."

ACKNOWLEDGMENTS

Many thanks to all the brilliant photographers who show us the incredible beauty of sea life. Special thanks to Jordan Harrison for the cover image.

PHOTO CREDITS

INDEX

Italic page numbers refer to illustrations.